VIRGO

SUN SIGN SERIES

Also by Joanna Martine Woolfolk

Sexual Astrology

Honeymoon for Life

The Only Astrology Book You'll Ever Need

VIRGO

SUN SIGN SERIES

JOANNA MARTINE WOOLFOLK

TAYLOR TRADE PUBLISHING
LANHAM • NEW YORK • BOULDER • TORONTO • PLYMOUTH, UK

Published by Taylor Trade Publishing
An imprint of The Rowman & Littlefield Publishing Group, Inc.
4501 Forbes Boulevard, Suite 200, Lanham, Maryland 20706
www.rlpgtrade.com

Estover Road, Plymouth PL6 7PY, United Kingdom

Distributed by National Book Network

British Library Cataloguing in Publication Information Available

Library of Congress Cataloging-in-Publication Data

Woolfolk, Joanna Martine.
Virgo / Joanna Martine Woolfolk.
p. cm.—(Sun sign series)
ISBN 978-1-58979-558-7 (pbk. : alk. paper)—ISBN 978-1-58979-533-4 (electronic)
1. Virgo (Astrology) I. Title.
BF1727.4.W66 2011
133.5'267—dc22 2011003354

∞™ The paper used in this publication meets the minimum requirements of American National Standard for Information Sciences—Permanence of Paper for Printed Library Materials, ANSI/NISO Z39.48-1992.

I dedicate this book to the memory of
William Woolfolk
whose wisdom continues to guide me,

and to
James Sgandurra
who made everything bloom again.

CONTENTS

ABOUT THE AUTHOR

Astrologer Joanna Martine Woolfolk has had a long career as an author, columnist, lecturer, and counselor. She has written the monthly horoscope for numerous magazines in the United States, Europe, and Latin America—among them *Marie Claire*, *Harper's Bazaar*, *Redbook*, *Self*, *YM*, *House Beautiful*, and *StarScroll International*. In addition to the best-selling *The Only Astrology Book You'll Ever Need*, Joanna is the author of *Sexual Astrology*, which has sold over a million copies worldwide, and *Astrology Source*, an interactive CD-ROM.

Joanna is a popular television and radio personality who has been interviewed by Barbara Walters, Regis Philbin, and Sally Jessy Raphael. She has appeared in a regular astrology segment on *New York Today* on NBC-TV and on *The Fairfield Exchange* on

CT Cable Channel 12, and she appears frequently on television and radio shows around the country. You can visit her website at www.joannamartinewoolfolk.com.

ACKNOWLEDGMENTS

Many people contribute to the creation of a book, some with ideas and editorial suggestions, and some unknowingly through their caring and love.

Among those who must know how much they helped is Jed Lyons, the elegant, erudite president of my publishers, the Rowman & Littlefield Publishing Group. Jed gave me the idea for this Sun Sign series, and I am grateful for his faith and encouragement.

Enormous gratitude also to Michael K. Dorr, my literary agent and dear friend, who has believed in me since we first met and continues to be my champion. I thank Michael for his sharp editor's eye and imbuing me with confidence.

Two people who don't know how much they give are my beloved sister and brother, Patricia G. Reynhout and Dr. John T. Galdamez. They sustain me with their unfailing devotion and support.

We are born at a given moment, in a given place,
and like vintage years of wine, we have the
qualities of the year and of the season
in which we are born.

Carl Gustav Jung

INTRODUCTION

When my publishers suggested I write a book devoted solely to Virgo, I was thrilled. I've long wanted to concentrate exclusively on your wonderful sign. You are very special in the zodiac. Astrology teaches that Virgo is the sign of excellence. Your sign represents intelligence, high standards, extraordinary commitment, and being a healing force. You are kindhearted and devoted, and your ability to *care for* is seen in everything you touch. In essence, Virgo is the *celestial craftsperson* who utilizes his or her inborn gifts to make the world more perfect. Karmic teachers say you were picked to be a Virgo because of your meritorious deeds of nurturing, love, and excellence in a previous life. But whether or not one believes in past lives, in *this* life you are Virgo, the splendid fixer who brings order and perfection.

These days it has become fashionable to be a bit dismissive of Sun signs (the sign that the Sun was in at the time of your birth). Some people sniff that "everyone knows about Sun signs." They say the descriptions are too "cookie-cutter," too much like cardboard figures, too inclusive (how can every Virgo be the same?).

Of course every Virgo is not the same! And many of these differences are not only genetic and environmental, but differences in your *charts*. Another Virgo would not necessarily have your Moon sign, or Venus sign, or Ascendant. However, these are factors to consider later—after you have studied your Sun sign. (In *The Only Astrology Book You'll Ever Need*, I cover in depth differences in charts: different Planets, Houses, Ascendants, etc.)

First and foremost, you are a Virgo. This is the sign the Sun was traveling through at the time of your birth.* The Sun is our most powerful planet. (In astrological terms, the Sun is referred to as a planet even though technically it is a "luminary.") It gives us life, warmth, energy, and food. It is the force that sustains us on Earth. The Sun is also the most important and pervasive influence in your horoscope and in many ways determines how others see you. Your Sun sign governs your individuality, your distinctive style, and your drive to fulfill your goals.

Your sign of Virgo symbolizes the role you are given to play in this life. It's as if at the moment of your birth you were pushed onstage into a drama called *This Is My Life*. In this drama, you are the starring actor—and Virgo is the character you play. What aspects of this character are you going to project? The Virgo integrity and dedication? Its amazing productivity, sense of style, ability to communicate? Or its bossiness, pettiness, and fault-finding ways? Your sign of Virgo describes your journey through this life, for it is your task to evolve into a perfect Virgo.

For each of us, the most interesting, most gripping subject is *self*. The longer I am an astrologer—which at this point is half my lifetime—the more I realize that what we all want to know is about ourselves. "Who am I?" you ask. You want to know what makes you tick, why you have such intense feelings, and whether

*From our viewpoint here on Earth, the Sun travels around the Earth once each year. Within the space of that year the Sun moves through all twelve signs of the zodiac, spending approximately one month in each sign.

others are also insecure. People ask me questions like "What kind of man should I look for?" "Why am I discontented with my job?" or "The man I'm dating is a Scorpio; will we be happy together?" They ask me if they'll ever find true love and when they will get out of a period of sadness or fear or the heavy burden of problems. They ask about their path in life and how they can find more fulfillment.

So I continue to see that the reason astrology exists is to answer questions about you. Basically, it's all about *you*. Astrology has been described as a stairway leading into your deeper self. It holds out the promise that you do not have to pass through life reacting blindly to experience, that you can within limits direct your own destiny and in the process reach a truer self-understanding.

Astrologically, the place to begin the study of yourself is your Sun sign. In this book, you'll read about your many positive qualities as well as your Virgo issues and negative inclinations. You'll find insights into your power and potentials, advice about love and sex, career guidance, health and diet tips, and information about myriads of objects, places, concepts, and things to which Virgo is attached. You'll also find topics not usually included in other astrology books—such as how Virgo fits in with Chinese astrology and with numerology.

Come with me on this exploration of the "infinite variety" (in Shakespeare's phrase) of being a Virgo.

Joanna Martine Woolfolk
Stamford, Connecticut
June 2011

VIRGO

AUGUST 23–SEPTEMBER 22

VIRGO.
Pl. 21.
BOOTES
COMA BERENICES
MONS MÆNALUS
LIBRA
NOCTUA
HYDRA
CORVUS
CRATER
LEO
Algorab

PART ONE

ALL ABOUT YOU

ILLUMINATING QUOTATIONS

"We are all pencils in the hand of God."

—Mother Theresa, Catholic nun and humanitarian, a Virgo

"I hear and I forget. I see and I remember. I do and I understand."

—Confucius, Chinese philosopher, a Virgo

"To achieve great things, two things are needed: a plan, and not quite enough time."

—Leonard Bernstein, composer, a Virgo

"We are born charming, fresh, and spontaneous, and must be civilized before we are fit to participate in society."

—Judith Martin (Miss Manners), etiquette expert, a Virgo

"Even in the valley of the shadow of death, two and two do not make six."

—Leo Tolstoy, novelist, a Virgo

"It is my belief we developed language because of our deep inner need to complain."

—Lily Tomlin, actress and comedienne, a Virgo

YOUR VIRGO PERSONALITY

YOUR MOST LIKEABLE TRAIT: Conscientiousness

The bright side of Virgo: Intellectual, meticulous, industrious, helpful, steadfast, responsible

The dark side of Virgo: Critical, high-strung, standoffish, argumentative, disapproving, hypochondriac

Your life's purpose is to be useful. You're caring and giving, practical and discriminating, industrious and painstaking—seeking to know and understand. Born at the time of the harvest, you're the one who separates the wheat from the chaff, the useful from the pointless, the valuable from the damaging, the healthy from the unhealthy. You have moral integrity and intellectual strength. You're extremely helpful and kind, yet your sensitive, tender side can be difficult to access until you feel safe. You take your time learning to trust another person. Because your nature is to perfect, you find flaws everywhere and are quick to point them out. You can be fussy and pedantic, and your perfectionism tends to drive others to distraction.

Yours is the sign of hidden emotion—the real drama of Virgo's personality is interior. To the world you may give an impression of calm authority and even seem remote and unreachable, for the quintessential Virgo has a serene, almost classic repose. But inwardly your emotions are surging. A great deal of nervous energy churns beneath the surface. You're always aware of your own restless, controlled intensity, the desire to be up and doing, rearranging, *improving*. Getting things done is a mania with you. You can exhaust yourself more by simply sitting still than others do moving around, and you have more energy than three people combined.

The planet Mercury, which rules both Virgo and Gemini, inclines its subjects toward constant activity. However, in Gemini the nervous energy is directed primarily toward stimulation and adventure, while in Virgo the ceaseless drive is to accomplish and perfect. It's important for Virgo not to put off until tomorrow what might be done today, or to do later what might be done now. You don't talk about what needs to be done—you go and do it. Your idea of taking it easy would seem like hard work to most people. You're not a daydreamer, you're a day-*doer*. You're happiest when your energies are engaged at full tilt.

Born with superlative gifts, you're known for your intelligence and razor-sharp perceptions. You're methodical, orderly, and efficient and have an excellent memory. In any project, you're likely to end up handling the major share of the responsibility because of your organizational abilities and mastery of detail. You are systematic, thorough, and painstaking. Famous for being a perfectionist, you pick, pick, pick (it keeps you calm). You set very high standards for yourself and insist that everyone around you toe the mark. If you fuss too much about details, it's because you believe a thing should be done right or not at all. You are both an artist and a craftsperson.

Your emotional life is a constant striving to bring order out of chaos. Although you have a great capacity for love, love alone is not enough for you to be happy. You need more than a mate, home, children, friends. You must justify your life, conduct yourself as a good bookkeeper keeps a ledger—always ready to give a reckoning on whether there's a profit or a loss. You're ambitious, but not just for money. You want to know more, to gain in wisdom, and put this wisdom to practical use. This practical realism makes you good at business and at handling money.

Indeed, the first thing you learned about money matters is that money does matter. Although you tend to downplay your own ability in financial affairs, no one is better at staying within a budget. You aren't tempted into foolish ventures. Your bank balances usually jibe to the decimal point. You want the finest but rarely overpay, and you have a built-in resistance against self-indulgence.

In the zodiac, Virgo is represented as a Virgin (or Maiden) holding a sheaf of wheat. Virgo is linked to the harvest. You take what has been sown (knowledge, information, skills) and harvest this energy to do something of practical benefit. In the same way wheat is turned into bread to feed our bodies, you want to utilize your inborn gifts to nourish the world. The Virgin does not mean you're a prude or lack sensuality—the Virgin stands for purity of purpose. Yours is the sign of work, duty, and service, and you find your satisfaction in giving yourself to others. Your true calling lies in service.

People do not always realize how much of your effort is directed toward helping others. This may be because on first meeting you tend to be somewhat aloof, careful about revealing too much of yourself to strangers. Yet almost immediately people see how crystal clear your thinking is. Those around you like to check their plans with you before putting them into action because you have microscopic vision when it comes to detecting a flaw.

Your superb logic cuts through muddled thinking like a laser beam. You instantly zero in on a problem, take apart difficulties, and put them back together in proper order. You find it frustrating to deal with minds that are illogical and scatterbrained. You value accuracy and are without peer in solving knotty problems or tangled disputes.

You believe life should be approached rationally and are convinced that a reasoned presentation of the facts will carry the day. Until you have the facts before you, you are reluctant to make a decision. Your immediate reaction to anything new is to analyze it; you want to know why and how a thing will work. Your faith is not in fortune cookies but in facts, and you distrust vague ideas that don't stand up to critical appraisal or people who make emotional judgments.

Yet it would do you a world of good to have a little more faith in general and to trust in synchronicity—that certain events occur or people connect for a fortuitous reason. Your important life lesson is to *expand your vision*, to look at things in larger terms and believe in the power of faith. Virgo is ruled by Mercury, the planet of thoughts and mental perceptions, and your ideas form your reality. If you hold on to a negative attitude, then your reality will also unfold negatively.

You tend to have difficulty getting in touch with your deeper feelings because your mechanism of denial is so firmly set in place. "I'm not upset," you'll say. "I feel okay about [this other person being promoted instead of me, his dating another woman, etc.]." Saying you feel "okay" covers a lot of messy feelings you'd rather not examine.

Also, you often don't see the forest for the trees. A preoccupation with neatness and precision sometimes limits your breadth of vision. That estimable faith in logic also confines your imagination and leaves you a little shy on inspiration, too dependent on established practices and methods. Your nature is to look back and analyze rather than push forward in a new direction. You must know the why and how of everything. Still, Virgo is a Mutable sign, and once you find a way of fitting the new situation into your routine, you can adjust easily to change.

You may run into difficulty because of a tendency to complicate everything. No problem is ever simple for Virgo. For every answer you've got a question, and making mountains out of molehills is one of your specialties.

A highly developed sense of discrimination may lead you to be hypercritical. You are unsatisfied with things as they are and continue to analyze situations and people in the hope of finding a way to make them better. At times your finely tuned sensibilities can make you unhappy, for they give you a heightened awareness of the world's imperfections. However, you resist criticism of your faults from others. It's a rare Virgo who takes criticism well or who can admit to being in the wrong.

You focus on mastering the small detail, as if this will keep you safe from the larger chaos of a random world. You become the victim of a deadening routine, of duty and discipline and a self-created regimented routine. You will accept a lesser role than you deserve because it's safer to remain an underling than reach out for power and risk failing. It's simpler to follow the rules and deal with black and white ("this is the right way, this is the wrong way").

Virgo is prone to depression born of feeling overlooked and undervalued, which Virgo has accepted to begin with because it's less challenging—and then feeling victimized by others. You see yourself as the "other," the one slighted, passed over, and taken advantage of.

On its deepest level, your turned-off attitude is the fear of being rejected. Yet you tend to bring on the very rejection you fear. You close yourself off and feel powerless. You become more critical, crabbed, and angry. You feel superior, yet also inferior (a sad and painful emotional conflict), and in this negative cycle, you drive others away from you.

Yet shining through everything is the fact that you're a giver. Basically you are kind, devoted, and very loyal. It may be hard for you to relax, to make small talk or be gregarious with strangers, but you're wonderful at friendships. You're far more comfortable in one-on-one encounters than with crowds. Here you can offer the full benefit of your sharp insights and discerning opinions, and this is when people discover how well-read, perceptive, charming, and witty you are. Warm, loving relationships bring out your best. When your affections are engaged you tirelessly try to serve. Loved ones will never have to worry about who is going to keep the checkbook balanced or look after them when they are ill.

THE INNER YOU

You have plenty of willpower and dedication, and you work harder than anyone to make sure something is perfect. Why? Because if you can't do everything superbly, you begin to fear that you're failing. You are much too critical of yourself. Actually, you're an enigma that no one has quite figured out. You hold back with people you don't know well and are reserved even with those you love. There's a part of yourself you'll always keep private. It's said that in ancient Egypt, the face of the Sphinx was modeled after Virgo—and the Sphinx is still an apt image for you, a person of secrets. Intensity and extreme sensitivity are part of those secrets. You feel very deeply and are very vulnerable. You can easily be hurt by a rebuff or a careless word, and rejection causes you such pain you put up a tough front that isn't easy to pierce. You're happiest looking after others—giving advice to friends, feeding stray animals, tending sick plants—but you need to be appreciated for the kind things you do. Above all, you want to be useful because you truly care about people.

HOW OTHERS SEE YOU

You're regarded as a real go-getter. People trust you to handle any job. They think of you as a person who is methodical in your thinking and can analyze almost any problem in a logical way. Others come to you when they want their own actions explained to them, or are feeling confused about relationships. You are valued for your ability to set priorities and create order out of confusion. Because you're both discriminating and truthful, people trust your judgment on books, theater, and clothes. However, you don't wear your heart on your sleeve, and as a result others often perceive you as haughty and cold.

GUARD AGAINST: Criticizing, Nagging, Fault-Finding

You are task oriented and detail minded, but so absorbed in making sure each little thing is perfect that you lose sight of the big picture (the whole project, the larger work of art, the interaction between people, and certainly others' feelings). You're quick to seize on people's mistakes and point out shortcomings. You carp, nitpick, and censor, and put a damper on other's efforts. You dole out criticism instead of compliments, negativity instead of praise. You can easily become a petty tyrant. In your exacting view, the world operates on "rules," and you expect people to follow the rules.

Moreover, coexisting with your instinct to give and to serve is a mistrusting nature that has a hard time delegating or believing others are as smart as you. Your attitude is that you're the expert who knows it all. But this creates internal conflict because you also suffer from insecurity. You think relying on rules and facts and being exact and perfect will keep you safe from error and failure.

Virgo, you need to lift your eyes and see that you hobble yourself with this constricted view. The boundaries you put on yourself keep you from forming loving and authentic bonds with others—and from performing with the imaginative brilliance you truly possess. You need to see the difference between faultfinding and evaluating (which you are marvelous at). You need to learn that perfectionism focuses on what's wrong, while excellence focuses on what's right. Your great Virgo gift is you're capable of bringing excellence to what you do.

YOUR GREATEST CHALLENGE:
To Not Take on the Role of the Martyr

It's Virgo's job to assume responsibility. You were born to be useful—to enhance, improve, and fix. Often you get into situations in which your helpfulness is taken advantage of, and much of the time you're the one who chooses these scenarios. Those who continually mess up or willfully use others seem to instinctively find their way to your side. The dynamics between the user (them) and the giver (you) keep compounding. You give and give, and become more resentful and angry.

These bitter feelings only feed your tendency to focus on everything that can go wrong. In this pessimistic state of mind, you dwell on hurts from the past and on a future that will turn out negatively. The ills you take into your psyche can also turn into physical illness. You're a worrier to begin with, and your multiple anxieties can manifest in stress-related sickness.

Yet you have the capacity to steer clear of situations in which you're undervalued and to rise out of a narrow and negative world. You have superior talents and a creative, forceful intelligence, and with your Virgo analytical gifts are able to choose what's valuable. Astrology teaches that Virgo is a spiritual sign—you have transformative power. You're blessed with the ability to care and, if you allow it expression, great vision. You see what *can* be. Of all the signs, you're the one who can take many possibilities, many choices, and fashion them into a perfect result.

YOUR ALTER EGO

Astrology gives us many tools in our lives to help manage our struggles and solve problems. One of these tools is to reach into your opposite sign in the zodiac—your polarity. For you, Virgo, this is Pisces, sign of fantasy, dreaming, intuition, and creativity. Pisces people rely on feelings; it is the prism through which they understand the world. Conversely, Virgo tends to filter all experience through the mind—and, specifically, through logic. You distrust emotion (and have a horror of emotional scenes). You're invested in solving problems rationally and making things work. In your mind, you see how facts fit together and, thus, you see the conclusion. But often you put the conclusion first, and if reality doesn't fall in line with your view, you're destabilized and distressed. Your insistence on being analytical blocks a natural flow of feelings between you and others, which causes you pain.

Pisces is always in the flow of feelings. Pisces intuitively senses the emotional climate, the unspoken words. In dealing with others Pisceans use insight and empathy, and as a result form close bonds. They are far more able than Virgo to live with ambiguity and the unexplainable. The signs of Virgo and Pisces are both Mutable, which means you're both flexible. But you're an Earth sign and the side-paths you explore are supposed to lead you to a real purpose. Pisces is a Water sign, happy to swim off in whatever direction the currents take it. Pisces never comes up short on imagination, and never gets stuck in insisting something must be so when it obviously isn't. For many Pisceans, the focus of their energies is to escape from rules and routine and the mundane.

By tapping into Pisces's open-ended view of life, you can release your Virgo creativity. When you move away from being a servant, and instead serve your own abilities, you'll find inspiration everywhere. Your mental dexterity and wide-ranging intellectual interests will be lit by new ideas. When you try an untried project, you'll no longer feel unappreciated and wasted. Above all, when you're comfortable with expressing feelings, you'll foster the emotional closeness you crave.

In turn, Pisces can learn highly important lessons from you in how not to drift off into escapism and dissipate its talents. Pisces tends to see real life as bondage because it isn't magical enough. You see real life as the place in which to fulfill your destiny. In the Kabbalah, Virgo is the sign "always busy doing the work of God." Pisces can use your discipline and commitment to excellence. And certainly it can benefit from knowing, as you do, how to live purposefully!

VIRGO IN LOVE

You distrust and are a little afraid of emotion. To you it represents the unknown, turbulent sea on which you may be set adrift without map or compass or rudder. Because of this, others may wonder if you're unfeeling. No, indeed! You're very sensitive, receptive, sensuous—and you long for love and companionship. But you're cautious about becoming involved with someone. You keep the vulnerable part of yourself hidden.

Others are aware that there are deeper wells of feeling in you. In fact, that mysteriousness is a powerful source of your allure. But even if you're wildly attracted to someone, you have an aloofness. Your eyes and body may say "come close," but your manner puts up a shield.

One reason is that you would never stoop to being obvious. You have a gentility about you and are as discriminating as you are careful. Virgo woman will wait for Mr. Right to come along, and meanwhile her off-putting manner serves a useful purpose. It keeps Mr. Wrong from intruding where he is not wanted. Virgo man would never sweep a woman into the bedroom and take her by force. He has too much respect for a woman.

Virgo is an Earth sign, and like all the Earth signs (Taurus, Virgo, Capricorn) you're an enigmatic combination of sensuality and conservatism. As a sign, Virgo itself is misunderstood. You're often characterized as timid, evasive, reserved. This is untrue. What Virgo has is self-possession, a sense of passion controlled by discipline.

The real clue to understanding your amorous nature is that you believe in true love. To you, saying yes with your heart is a commitment to a future together. Therefore, you fear being trapped in a long-term living arrangement with the wrong person. Before you marry or enter into a meaningful affair, you're careful to note where the exit doors are. Falling in love can take a long time. You move forward step by step, revealing the layers of your deep sensitivity, learning to trust.

But once you feel safe and secure in a relationship, your radiance can light up a room. When your emotions are unlocked your enormous capacity for loving pours out from a rich treasury. In love, you shed your reserve. You reveal your deep sensuality and become a rich, exciting, passionate lover. You're endlessly willing to experiment with sexual techniques that heighten the ecstasy. In addition, you offer lifelong dividends of love and loyalty. *Fidelity* is not just a word to you. No one could have a mate more generous and giving, a lover, friend, and ally for all seasons.

Still, the human heart is complicated, and yours is no exception. Virgo takes relationships very seriously but, prudent as you may think you are, you don't always make wise choices in love. Because of her own emotional reticence, Virgo woman is not skilled at recognizing a man playing at love. She can be consumed by glamorous excitement and electrifying passion, and the end of that story is heartbreak. Virgo man has a horror of getting embroiled in stormy scenes and angry tantrums, yet is drawn to tempestuous women. Emotionality upsets him but, because he's both attracted to it and disturbed by it, his love life never runs as smoothly as he'd like.

Also, even at the beginning of a relationship, problems tend to arise because of your hidden list. A lover must be sincere, accomplished, neat, and well-read, and have good prospects and serious purpose. What is on your list is fine, but your criteria tend to be rigid and you're too judgmental. It's obvious this doesn't leave much room for fun. And you can miss out on love blossoming with someone who doesn't fit your "conditions" but would be perfect for you.

Another love mistake is you tend to become the martyr in a relationship. Paradoxically Virgo, who is so good at self-containment, is the sign of selflessness. You need to be needed, and can easily become enmeshed with someone who is very needy. Sometimes you feel sorry for the person; sometimes you give of yourself to get love. And in your resentment at being the one who does the giving, you never see your own responsibility in what went wrong. You have a hard time looking into yourself. Nor are you good at letting go and moving on. You hold on to the wrong things too long.

Hidden resentment in a relationship can also turn you into something of a tyrant. In public you are kind and helpful, but in private you can be a petty dictator. Yes, you're very giving in a relationship, but you become angry if your partner doesn't fall in line with your rules. You can turn cold. You operate from very deep defenses.

However, within you is also a deep desire to break out of Virgo imprisonments. You'd like to change your image. Virgo woman can see herself as a sophisticated seductress, a femme fatale. Virgo man would like to be a love-'em-and-leave-'em type, a Don Juan, a bon vivant. The one who taps into this secret fantasy will reap the surprisingly rich and memorable rewards of your Virgo pent-up sensuality. It's all there under the surface, and it's the kind of sensuality that improves with time.

Love frees you to be the true you—joyful, effervescent, fully alive. It unlocks your passion, your loyalty, and the secret depths of your eroticism. Bottom line, love means a promise to be there.

Your outstanding characteristic in a relationship is your need to benefit your lover—you're a helpmate in every sense of the word. What you want is an intimate, achieving, working partnership that enables you both to open yourselves to whatever adventures life may bring and scale new heights together.

TIPS FOR THOSE WHO WANT TO ATTRACT VIRGO

The rule to bear in mind is this: Don't overpower. Underplay.

Always try to be a good sport. If that drink you're invited for turns out to be at a health-food store and consists of carrot and cucumber juice, smile and gulp it. Virgos are finicky eaters and careful about their health. With them, the laws of nutrition rate just behind the Ten Commandments.

In addition to the old standby of discussing work-connected topics, another good conversational subject is pets. Virgos like the smaller variety, especially the exotic kind.

Quickly establish your cultural credentials. Virgos are drawn to people whose intelligence or learning is superior to their own.

Don't probe too closely into their personal affairs. They guard their private life. Avoid noisy places or entertainment that is vulgar or offensive. Virgos pride themselves on their good taste.

Don't let Virgo's worrying upset you. People born under this sign are natural worriers. Will they be on time for the show? Will they catch the plane? Will it rain or snow? Will the check they're expecting arrive? The list of their worries is endless. It's no use pointing out that most of the things they worry about never actually happen. They'll go right on worrying anyway; it's their way of coping with what *might* go wrong.

Both male and female Virgos appreciate gifts that are useful and practical. They are also great hobbyists and are sure to have at least one particular interest.

Very few special occasions with Virgo will occur on the spur of the moment—at least not if Virgo can help it. There will be careful planning; all the moves will be figured out in advance. Virgo is marvelous at working behind the scenes to accomplish this. All you have to do is relax and enjoy it.

VIRGO'S EROGENOUS ZONES: Tips for Those with a Virgo Lover

Our bodies are very sensitive to the touch of another human being. The special language of touching is understood on a level more basic than speech. Each sign is linked to certain zones and areas of the body that are especially receptive and can receive sexual messages through touch. Many books and manuals have been written about lovemaking, but few pay attention to the unique knowledge of erogenous zones supplied by astrology. You can use astrology to become a better, more sensitive lover.

As a prelude to making love with a Virgo, a playful tête-à-tête in the bath is just the thing to please. One reason: Virgo is very attracted to cleanliness. While in the bath, gently lave Virgo's stomach area with a sponge, soap, and warm water. For Virgoans, the entire stomach area is responsive to erotic touching, kissing, and stroking. They also enjoy the feeling of a spray of warm water over this area. A handheld shower nozzle will do the trick nicely.

In bed it is very easy to arouse Virgo sexually with this massage: (1) Begin by slowly and gently stroking the abdomen, starting just under the chest and going down to the top of the legs. Use your fingertips and cover the entire area. (2) Using a featherlight touch, stroke long lines from the navel to the genitals with your fingertip. Do the same thing using just fingernails and scarcely touching flesh. (3) Moving in a large circle, stroke the stomach area with your fingertips, describing smaller and smaller circles until you are at the rim of the navel.

By this time Virgo is your slave.

VIRGO'S AMOROUS COMBINATIONS: YOUR LOVE PARTNERS

VIRGO AND ARIES

You're drawn to Aries's energy and high spirits. Aries is fun, smart, on the ball, willing to try anything, and you're intrigued by its audaciousness. Soon, though, your prudent ways clash with Aries's over-the-top personality that quickly becomes annoying. As a couple you two have difficulty communicating because Virgo wants to talk and Aries wants to act. Your arguments will probably be more passionate than your lovemaking. Aries will think you inhibited; you will consider Aries impulsive and wild—not to mention sexually selfish. Socially, Aries likes a lively, flamboyant scene with lots of animated people and parties. You are happy with cozy dinners at home with intellectually stimulating friends. Aries is also the type to bring out your worst habits of nitpicking and nagging. Exit romance.

VIRGO AND TAURUS

You are analytical while Taurus is sensuous, but Taurus's strong passions can spark you. If this happens, you make lovely love, for you bring out each other's romanticism. Also, the earthy sexuality you share leads you into deeper emotional intimacy. Because you two have much in common, you understand each other's needs. You're both homebodies, you have similar intellectual and artistic tastes, and you both want a stable, *non*chaotic life. Practical, down-to-earth, and satisfied with the tried-and-true, you both try to build for a secure future. Virgo's rational approach and Taurus's persistence are also a good moneymaking combination, an added plus since you're likely to develop a business idea together. The cornerstone in this relationship is the fact that you're able to depend on each other. Auguries couldn't be more promising.

VIRGO AND GEMINI

You're attracted to one another because of a mutual interest in intellectual ideas. Both of you have active minds—but you use your intelligence to deal with the world rationally, whereas Gemini is far more interested in expressing itself. Gemini enjoys a crowd, you like one-on-one. Your temperaments are too unalike to sustain any initial mental rapport. Gemini is excitable, scattered, and spontaneous; you are methodical, organized, and cautious. As a duo you ratchet up the irritability level in each other. In matters of sex, Gemini's nature is too impulsive and unstable to suit you. Gemini dismisses you as a stick-in-the-mud. You consider Gemini irresponsible and adolescent. Gemini needs freedom to pursue its varied interests. You resent this and will nag and try to dominate. Gemini will soon stray.

VIRGO AND CANCER

A stimulating affair, for you arouse each other's beneath-the-surface sensuality. You both need to feel safe in order to be freely passionate, and together you create the perfect romantic climate. Cancer isn't too forceful, which suits you fine—and the little attentions won't be neglected by Cancer, which you like even better. Cancer is affectionate and sentimental and makes you feel cherished. As a couple you have much in common. You both like money and domestic comfort, and your career goals mesh well. Emotionally, too, Cancer's dependency fits perfectly with your protectiveness. You have an efficient way of smoothing out problems so that your lives maintain a sense of order. On the downside, you both tend to be overcritical. On the upside, you each draw the other out of its shell.

VIRGO AND LEO

At the beginning, Leo's larger-than-life exuberance seizes your attention, and in turn Leo is charmed by your quick mind. But the moment you two become sexually involved, highly physical Leo takes it as a personal affront if you don't match its leonine ardor. Your reserved nature frustrates Leo and leads to quarrels. You are not quick to hand out praise, and Leo lives on nothing but. Leo is a spendthrift; you are careful with pennies. Both of you are independent, but Leo exhibits this in a temperamental way, while you are very private. Though you're a born helper, when Leo imperiously starts giving orders you become obstinate and refuse to lift a finger. You simply will not be dominated by tyrannical Leo and always have your guard up. This affair has a shorter life than a mayfly.

VIRGO AND VIRGO

All is smooth sailing as long as you two perfectionists curb your instincts for finding fault. Actually, you bring out the best in each other. You are responsible, sensitive, and intelligent, and you take love seriously. You each have an empathetic understanding of the other (karmic teachers say you two came together to heal past hurts). You also share passions of the mind and will never bore one another. You both think there are more important things in life than sex; you may end up just talking in bed. You need to consciously introduce fun and recreation into your lives because you are doers and achievers—and two Virgos together are doubly focused on goals. There will probably be a continual contest over who is leader, but you have too much else in common for this to matter.

VIRGO AND LIBRA

Libra is too frivolous and shallow for your tastes. Libra tends to inhabit a glamorous world that it busily fashions—Libra enjoys spending money, going to parties, and being the center of attention. You criticize, and this makes Libra feel unloved. Libra may tap your hidden sensuality, but Virgo and Libra personalities are altogether too different for real compatibility. Although you're both partnership oriented, the things each of you looks for in an alliance are at odds. You want a working partnership that creates stability. Libra longs for a romantic bonding that fills its fantasies. You will try to curb and dominate Libra's fickle and outer-directed nature. You are reserved and practical, and Libra views this as a personal rebuff. Libra will soon drift away in search of more fun-loving companions.

VIRGO AND SCORPIO

Sensual Scorpio keeps trying to entice you into ever-bolder sexual adventures. But you're pleased because Scorpio is also possessive and fiercely loyal, which makes you feel loved and protected. Your passion together is only part of the hidden emotional/intellectual depth in your relationship. You definitely admire each other's minds. Virgo is logical, intellectual, analytical. Scorpio is imaginative visionary, and perceptive. Part of the chemistry between you is an intense drive to be successful. An issue to work on is that each of you sometimes has trouble verbalizing real feelings. Scorpio is volatile but secretive; Virgo is self-restrained and reserved. There also may be some conflict about which one of you runs things, but your Virgo willingness to compromise keeps Scorpio tractable.

VIRGO AND SAGITTARIUS

You two are like the grasshopper and the ant. Sagittarius's free spirit has nothing in common with hardworking, diligent Virgo. Sagittarius has a reckless gambler's attitude, while you carefully build for future security. You see the glass as half empty, and you strive to fill it. Sagittarius sees it as half full and rising rapidly. Both of you are intellectual signs, but the way Sagittarius's mind works clashes with the way yours works. Sagittarius is expansive and extravagant, while you prefer a simple, ordered, and unpretentious life. You're both brutally honest; Sagittarius is tactless and you're critical, so communication between you has sharp edges. Sagittarius considers your sexual attitudes rather prudish and won't stay long in one bedroom anyway.

VIRGO AND CAPRICORN

A harmonious pairing. Capricorn's ambition and drive for success meshes well with your Virgo perfectionism and energy. Both of you are diligent and disciplined and have a sense of purpose. Money cheers you, and hard work is the order of the day. Virgo and Capricorn are both Earth signs, and as a couple you want to be on solid ground—financially and emotionally. You admire one another and take great pride in pleasing each other. You both need respect and approval (though neither of you will confess this), and each gives to the other exactly that. Deep down, both of you are romantics—the only thing is, you need to make time for romance or it will slip by you. Sexual compatibility is all there, and together you find true mutual passion. In lovemaking, though, Capricorn usually takes the lead.

VIRGO AND AQUARIUS

If relationships were purely an intellectual exercise, you and Aquarius would have the intellect to make yours work. Both of you are cerebral and rational and tend to view love in the abstract. However, the similarity ends there. Aquarius has venturesome ideas and thinks you unresponsive or cold. Actually, each of you has a distant quality: You are cautious about emotional giving; Aquarius's thoughts are in the far-off clouds. Aquarius is interested in other people, in causes, and in setting the world right. You seek personal achievement and financial security. Aquarius is outgoing, inventive, a visionary. You are reserved, prudent, and very practical about your ambitions. Also, there's little sexual rapport, for each of you tends to push away the other when you're feeling in conflict. As a twosome you may not even make it as friends.

VIRGO AND PISCES

To you, love means security and mental compatibility. To Pisces, love is a sweeping, all-enveloping emotion. At first you two are powerfully attracted to each other—as opposites in the zodiac often are. You're very intrigued by sentimental, in-love-with-love Pisces, and Pisces is fascinated by your incisive, analytical Virgo mind. However, disillusion quickly sets in. Pisces's extravagance, secretiveness, and dreaminess frustrate a pragmatic, orderly, logical Virgo. The more you try to enlighten Pisces with a dash of common sense, the more eccentrically Pisces behaves. You want to deal with problems rationally whereas Pisces wants to escape from them. Sexually, everything is too hyper and chaotic for you—you want intimacy, not soap opera—and you're highly unlikely to adapt to some of Pisces's erotic preferences.

YOUR VIRGO CAREER PATH

You were born to be the fixer, the one who serves and helps and makes things perfect. Therefore, your career must give you the feeling you're setting the world aright. You do not necessarily have to be in political life or missionary work but, for you to be fulfilled, what you do must have an element of service. This does not mean being a *servant*—it means serving your wonderful talents.

Indeed, you are multitalented and, more than this, a superb craftsperson. Had you been born in a previous century, you would have been the one who carved and painted and created one-of-a-kind works of art. Much of your Virgo passion is expressed through work—and you need to choose wisely so that your labors are about something you love. As the philosophical author Khalil Gibran wrote, "Work is love made visible," and this is certainly true for you.

Drudgery will eat away at your soul.

Virgo has a reputation for being a slave to routine. But a fine line exists between being disciplined and ordered—following a routine—and locking yourself into repetitive monotony. Learn the difference, and you will thrive. The ancient adage, "Discipline and freedom are inseparable," is a motto for Virgo.

It's true that being organized is your method to finding the freedom to create. For you to work in chaos is painful; it blocks your thinking processes and destroys your creativity. Everything in you tries to prevent disarray. Thus, you should be in charge of how a project is coordinated and the one who handles the details and does the final check-through so that you have the most control when the unexpected happens. It's crucial to recognize that your nagging sense that something will go wrong hampers you, becomes a weight you carry, and will lead to a dark resignation that the world is negative. Remember, you alone have the power to banish this Virgo bugaboo.

Because you're efficient and task oriented, you tend to land in positions where you assist. This is fine to start with; you learn the inner workings of a business this way, and how to run an enterprise. Unquestionably you're a quick learner—Mercury endows you with brilliant brainpower. You're also highly principled and precise, and have excellent timing. You are canny with money and able to manage people. In short, you have leadership skills, and one of your most important career lessons is to *value* your work and not be reluctant to keep rising to higher levels.

This is not to say that being an assistant is lowly. No, indeed, your ability to direct and execute is among your brilliant skills. It's that being Virgo, you demand perfection of yourself and are shadowed by a fear of failure. You find it easier to ask for more work than to ask for a promotion. Your challenge is to not allow your fear to keep you in subservient positions in which you settle for security, waste your talents on the mediocre, and let your magnificent potential go unrealized.

Your ruling planet Mercury presides over intellectual activities, speech, and writing. You're an idea person, thoughtful and analytical, and you shine in the field of communication. Your talent for fact-finding and dealing with information enables you to be a good editor, teacher, or librarian, or a researcher or scientist. The cosmic job of Virgo is to take what is harvested (knowledge, news, information) and put this to practical use, and writing and journalism are fields that utilize this skill. Virgo's *service* is to nourish others—to do work that nurtures the mind or body—and the concept of *health* is very much a part of Virgo's symbolism. Thus, you're drawn to professions that help people, for example, a career in medicine, nursing, social work, or the law. The sign of Virgo is linked to small animals and you have a special gift for veterinary medicine. You are a sympathetic adviser, and well suited for work in vocational and psychological counseling. You also have an aptitude for computer technology and finance, which may lead you into a cutting-edge business career.

Others think you're lucky in the workplace because you seem to get what you want. But it is *you* who makes this happen. You're blessed in that you enjoy work, and throughout your life people will offer you jobs out of the blue because you can handle anything. Most important, you're willing to work for what you want, and so you get it.

The secret to finding your career bliss is threefold: Make sure your work contributes to the well-running of an enterprise and well-being of others. Be passionate about what you do. Value yourself—without you, the world would be a poorer place.

VIRGO AND HEALTH: ADVICE FROM ASTROLOGY

For optimum health, Virgo must learn how to deal with the abundance of nervous energy that is the birthright of your sign. You are a doer, go-getter, achiever, and worrier. Your life runs on a timetable, and being behind schedule causes anxiety. You're also busy handling details and fretting about what can go wrong. Born under the sign of well-being, you have an instinct for how to take care of yourself. But you must put this into practice. You're especially prone to ailments involving the stomach, intestines, and bowels. Stress and tension play havoc with your digestive system, as well as cause skin disorders and allergies. Your major key to good health is to find ways to calm your mind. You need to eat nutritiously, and develop a program of exercise, recreation, and rest that keeps you centered.

Advice and useful tips about health are among the most important kinds of information that astrology provides. Health and well-being are of paramount concern to human beings. Love, money, or career take second place, for without good health we cannot enjoy anything in life.

Astrology and medicine have had a long marriage. Hippocrates (born around 460 B.C.), the Greek philosopher and physician who is considered the father of medicine, said, "A physician without a knowledge of astrology has no right to call himself a physician." Indeed, up until the eighteenth century, the study of astrology and its relationship to the body was very much a part of a doctor's training. When a patient became ill, a chart was immediately drawn up. This guided the doctor in both diagnosis and treatment, for the chart would tell when the crisis would come and what medicine would help. Of course, modern Western doctors no longer use astrology to treat illness. However, astrology can still be a useful tool in helping to understand and maintain our physical well-being.

THE PART OF THE BODY RULED BY VIRGO

Each sign of the zodiac governs a specific part of the body. These associations date back to the beginning of astrology. Curiously, the part of the body that a sign rules is in some ways the strongest and in other ways the weakest area for natives of that sign.

Your sign of Virgo rules the nervous system and the intestines. The intestines assimilate food into the body. By the same token, you assimilate knowledge and turn it into practical use. You have a delicate and finely turned nervous system, which makes you intuitive and discriminating.

As with Cancer people, nervous tension, anxiety, and emotional stress are Virgo's worst enemies. You can literally worry yourself sick. When things go wrong, you have a tendency to turn the trouble in on yourself and the problem is instantly reflected in a physical ailment, usually intestinal.

You have a fussy digestive system and suffer from indigestion, gas pains, ulcers, liver upsets, colitis, and bowel problems. In addition, you're often troubled by skin eruptions, again due to nerves. On a positive note, Virgo is the zodiac sign that represents health and well-being, and you are therefore health-conscious. You try to make sure you get enough vitamins and go for regular checkups at the dentist. However, in this as in other areas, you can't help being a worrier, and hypochondria is common among Virgos.

Virgo's ruling planet Mercury has dominion over the brain and the nervous system. It also controls the links between the mind and the functions of the body. This intensifies your proclivity for turning mental tension and upsets into illness of the body.

DIET AND HEALTH TIPS FOR VIRGO

You have to coddle your sensitive digestive system. A proper diet is essential to good health and to keeping up energy. In addition, food should not be highly seasoned, spicy, laden with sauces or gravies, or fried.

The cell salt* for Virgo is potassium sulphate, which regulates oil in the body, carries oxygen to cells, and is essential to muscle contraction. This mineral keeps the pores of the skin unclogged and ventilated. Lack of potassium sulphate in the diet causes dandruff, hair loss, eczema, acne, and dry, flaky skin and hair. A deficiency also leads to extreme fatigue and constipation. Foods high in this necessary mineral are green leafy vegetables (endive,

**Cell salts* (also known as *tissue salts*) are mineral compounds found in human tissue cells. These minerals are the only substances our cells cannot produce by themselves. The life of cells is relatively short, and the creation of new cells depends on the presence of these minerals.

chicory, romaine), whole-wheat and whole-grain breads, wheat-germ oil, oats, almonds, cheese, oranges, bananas, lemons, lean beef, and lamb. Healthy foods that are easy to digest are corn bread, yogurt, brown rice, eggs, and cottage cheese.

Melons, apples, pears, and papaya are particularly good for you, and lemon juice in the diet will ease skin eruptions and dandruff. Honey should be used as a sweetener instead of sugar. Herb teas soothe delicate stomachs. Virgo loves chocolate, which unfortunately does not love you; it causes upsets of the skin and digestive system. You do not tolerate drugs well, and medicine should be taken only under a doctor's supervision.

Exercise is important for you, and exercises such as yoga and tai chi that combine body movement with a meditative aspect are especially good at reducing stress. You also need sunshine (in moderate amounts) and plenty of sound, restful sleep. Definitely schedule regular periods of relaxation—it's hard not to worry when one is a worrier, but it helps to get away from it all and think about something else.

THE DECANATES AND CUSPS OF VIRGO

Decanate and *cusp* are astrological terms that subdivide your Sun sign. These subdivisions further define and emphasize certain qualities and character traits of your Sun sign, Virgo.

WHAT IS A DECANATE?

Each astrological sign is divided into three parts, and each part is called a *decanate* or a *decan* (the terms are used interchangeably).

The word comes from the Greek word *dekanoi*, meaning "ten days apart." The Greeks took their word from the Egyptians, who divided their year into 360 days.* The Egyptian year had twelve months of thirty days each, and each month was further divided into three sections of ten days each. It was these ten-day sections that the Greeks called *dekanoi*.

*The Egyptians soon found out that a 360-day year was inaccurate, and so added on five extra days. These were feast days and holidays, and not counted as real days.

Astrology still divides the zodiac into decanates. There are twelve signs in the zodiac, and each sign is divided into three decanates. You might picture each decanate as a room. You were born in the sign of Virgo, which consists of three rooms (decanates). In which room of Virgo were you born?

The zodiac is a 360-degree circle. Each decanate is ten degrees of that circle, or about ten days long, since the Sun moves through the zodiac at approximately the rate of one degree per day. (This is not exact, because not all of our months contain thirty days.)

The decanate of a sign does not change the basic characteristics of that sign, but it does refine and individualize the sign's general characteristics. If you were born, say, in the second decanate of Virgo, it does not change the fact you are Virgo. It does indicate that you have somewhat special characteristics, different from those of Virgo people born in the first decanate or the third decanate.

Finally, each decanate has a specific planetary ruler, sometimes called a subruler because it does not usurp the overall rulership of your sign. The subruler can only enhance and add to the distinct characteristics of your decanate. For example, your entire sign of Virgo is ruled by Mercury, but the second decanate of Virgo is subruled by Saturn. The influence of Saturn, the subruler, combines with the overall authority of Mercury to make the second decanate of Virgo unlike any other in the zodiac.

FIRST DECANATE OF VIRGO

August 23 through September 1
Keyword: Analysis

Constellation: Crater, the Cup, the goblet of Apollo. The Cup symbolizes emotional giving.
Planetary subruler: Mercury

Mercury, planet of the mind, is both your ruler and subruler, giving you a formidable intellect. You approach problems rationally; you want to find out the reason things happen, and then apply your knowledge to working out a better system. Often your insights are thought of as prophetic, but they are the result of keen observation. You have a warm and witty personality that draws friends and admirers. However, your standards are high and you expect intelligence and decorum in the people with whom you associate. In love, you are romantic and devoted and have great sensitivity toward a lover. A great deal of nervous energy is churning beneath your surface. You tend to worry secretly and to fuss over small problems.

SECOND DECANATE OF VIRGO

September 2 through September 12
Keyword: Efficiency
Constellation: Hercules, the strong and virtuous hero who triumphed over evil.
Planetary subruler: Saturn

Saturn, planet of determination, combines with Virgo's Mercury to give special force to your personality. You are concerned with details and want to plot your moves in advance so there won't be any mistakes. Though you are versatile and adaptable, most people think of you as persistent and tenacious. Your fixity of purpose is simply that you demand perfection of yourself and try to give your best performance. In truth you are too exacting and suffer needlessly when you don't live up to your expectations. When you are in love you have a gentle and sympathetic nature, and you do all in your power to please. You are easy to live with as long as no one arouses your strong stubborn streak.

THIRD DECANATE OF VIRGO

September 13 through September 22

Keyword: Discrimination

Constellation: Bootes, the Bear Driver, the ancient herdsman who every day chased the Great Bear around the North Pole. Bootes symbolizes the utilization of knowledge.

Planetary subruler: Venus

The gregarious and social qualities of Venus combine with Virgo's Mercury to signify a winning way with people. What motivates you is a desire for approval. You have a special talent for using words and can write and speak charmingly. An artistic flair and use of color is usually present in your surroundings or dress. You possess a sense of style and project a strong personal image. Poise and confidence are assets in your work or career, and you are known for your tact and diplomacy. Since you are unhappy living under restrictions, you are drawn to creative pursuits where you are free to be your own master. In love, you are warmhearted and generous, though you demand a lot of attention in return.

WHAT IS A CUSP?

A *cusp* is the point at which a new astrological sign begins.* Thus, the cusp of Virgo means the point at which Virgo begins. (The word comes from the Latin word *cuspis*, meaning "point.")

When someone speaks of being "born on the cusp," that person is referring to a birth time at or near the beginning or the end of an astrological sign. For example, if you were born on September 22, you were born on the cusp of Libra, the sign that begins on September 23. Indeed, depending on what year you were born, your birth time might even be in the first degree of Libra. People born on the very day a sign begins or ends are often confused about what sign they really are—a confusion made more complicated by the fact that the Sun does not move into or out of a sign at *exactly* the same moment (or even day) each year. There are slight time differences from year to year. Therefore, if you are a Virgo born on August 23 or September 22, you'll find great clarity consulting a computer chart that tells you exactly where the Sun was at the very moment you were born.

As for what span of time constitutes being born on the cusp, the astrological community holds various opinions. Some astrologers claim *cusp* means being born only within the first two days or last two days of a sign (though many say this is too narrow a time frame). Others say it can be as much as within the first ten days or last ten days of a sign (which many say is too wide an interpretation). The consensus is that you were born on the cusp if your birthday is within the first *five* days or last *five* days of a sign.

*In a birth chart, a cusp is also the point at which an astrological House begins.

The question hanging over cusp-born people is, "What sign am I really?" They feel they straddle the border of two different countries. To some extent, this is true. If you were born on the cusp, you're under the influence of both signs. However, much like being a traveler leaving one country and crossing into another, you must actually *be* in one country—you can't be in two countries at the same time. One sign is always a stronger influence, and that sign is almost invariably the sign that the Sun was actually in (in other words, your Sun sign). The reason I say "almost" is that in rare cases a chart may be so heavily weighted with planets in a certain sign that the person more keenly feels the influence of that specific sign.

For example, I have a client who was born in the evening on September 22. On that evening, the Sun was leaving Virgo and entering Libra. At the moment of her birth the Sun was still in Virgo, so technically speaking she is a Virgo. However, the Sun was only a couple hours away from being in Libra, and this person has the Moon, Mercury, and Venus all in Libra. She has always felt like a Libran and always behaved as a Libran.

This, obviously, is an unusual case. Generally, the Sun is the most powerful planetary influence in a chart. Even if you were born with the Sun on the very tip of the first or last degree of Virgo, Virgo is your Sun sign—and this is the sign you will most feel like.

Still, the influence of the approaching sign or of the sign just ending is present, and you will probably sense that mixture in yourself.

BORN AUGUST 23 THROUGH AUGUST 27

You are Virgo with Leo tendencies. You are kind, gracious, and reliable, and you also possess great flair and personal style. Your optimism, wit, and sense of fun magnetically draw people toward you. Projects you undertake are likely to be successful because of your eye for detail and quick intelligence. Often you end up handling the whole show because of your organizational abilities. Sometimes you are impatient with the irresponsibility of others. You shine in social settings. In love, you tend to be effusive, warm, and loyal.

BORN SEPTEMBER 18 THROUGH SEPTEMBER 22

You are Virgo with Libra tendencies. You are an idea person, intellectual and perceptive. You have a gregarious nature and are most successful dealing with and through other people. Your mind is alert and lively, and you probably have a facile flair for conversation. Your particular gift is for using your social talents in your work. Your finely honed aesthetic sense sets high standards. You may be a collector of beautiful objects or be drawn to creative pursuits. In love, you are sincere and expressive but need a lot of attention and devotion from a lover.

YOUR SPECIAL DAY OF BIRTH

AUGUST 23

You're a "natural"—people are drawn to your easy, unaffected quality. You're also witty and highly intelligent, and born to create something important in the world. You have a wild romantic streak and can be a fool for love.

AUGUST 24

You're a leader and, unlike many Virgos, comfortable with change. You enjoy a mental challenge and are always ready for a fun adventure. You're ambitious and passionate, and a lover is never totally secure about you.

AUGUST 25

You have elegance and charm and, whatever your circumstance, give the impression of being born into wealth. New people and situations fuel your imagination. In love, you're flirtatious and deeply devoted at the same time.

AUGUST 26

You have the gift of seeing into others (some call you psychic), and are known as the wise one. You do best in an organized and aesthetic environment. In work, you're exacting, and in love, you give your heart with abandon.

AUGUST 27

There are paradoxes to you. You see the big picture yet have a penetrating eye for detail. You enjoy spontaneity, yet your cautious side usually makes you take your time deciding things. In love, though, you're true blue and powerfully passionate.

AUGUST 28

You have a zany sense of humor and are full of ideas and inspiration. Inwardly you may feel unsure, but outwardly you emanate great force of will. You have a strong creative streak and, when in love, are erotically ardent.

AUGUST 29

People see you as proud and dignified, yet you see yourself as a rebellious artist. What is true is that you're an intellectual, tastemaker, and sexual magnet all at the same time. In love, you need to manage your control issues so that you're easier to live with.

AUGUST 30

Early on, you must travel down some unusual byways until you find your calling. Your special talents will come together in an important project. You have strong loyalty and, in love, are a passionate romantic. Guard against a tendency to obsess.

AUGUST 31

People think you're charming, but you must also cope with strong up-and-down mood swings. You're content being left alone to create and not answering to anyone. Romantically, you want to believe in lasting love but one choice is bound to cause you heartbreak.

SEPTEMBER 1

You have a head for business and a heart for love—and a tendency to either overwork or be swept away by passion. You need to learn how to stay in balance. The second half of your life promises to be far more serene than the first.

SEPTEMBER 2

You can be fierce about your likes, loves, and ambitions, but have such elegant manners people don't always decipher your feelings. You have a dramatic presence and unusual career talents. Sexually, you're high combustion, and emotionally you have deep needs.

SEPTEMBER 3

You're wholehearted about what you do and strive for perfection, but you are also a fun-loving teaser. You can be curiously detached when your mind races on to the next new thing. In love, you need a special person who can match your high ideals.

SEPTEMBER 4

Your creative adrenaline works overtime—and your sharp mind is a laser beam that probes into information and other people's motivations. You're a bit distrustful in romantic affairs but after some trial and error will fall deeply in love.

SEPTEMBER 5

You have amazing energy, are easily bored, and need stimulation. You seek new knowledge, creative pursuits, and interesting people. Romantically, you have strong desires and must be careful not to become a love addict.

SEPTEMBER 6

You're an observer and listener, constantly analyzing people and situations. Because of your brilliance, you're powerful at what you do. In love, you need a best friend (deep mental affinity) and also lots of space.

SEPTEMBER 7

You have ingenuity and "people smarts," and are both an egalitarian and an elitist. In your work, you're a visionary who sees what others can't. Emotionally, you need *compassionate* love and high intelligence from a partner, a combination not easy to fill.

SEPTEMBER 8

You're independent, rational, communicative, and romantic—a lovely mix others often can't figure out. You're a strong individualist with a brilliant mind and "off the wall" talents. When you're deeply committed, you never let your lover down.

SEPTEMBER 9

You have a dramatic, creative personality, you're highly intuitive, and people see you as dominant. Like a wolf, you're devoted to your immediate "pack" and will do anything in your power to keep them safe. In love, your steadfastness is legendary.

SEPTEMBER 10

Your great strengths are your reasoning powers and cooperative spirit. Good career karma follows you—you can spot opportunity. Matters of the heart tend to be your Achilles heel. Perhaps you "love too much," yet the universe promises a soulmate.

SEPTEMBER 11

You live according to a personal moral code—others look to you to know the right thing to do. You're also quick, funny, and smart as a whip, and you have a connoisseur's eye for beauty. In love, you tend to give too much too soon.

SEPTEMBER 12

You're deeply imaginative, highly social, and beautifully eloquent. You've learned the hard way to draw the line before becoming the sacrificer. Romantic life can be complicated because of your magnetic sexuality and hungry heart.

SEPTEMBER 13

Your offhand manner belies a sensitive and sentimental heart. Creatively, you surprise people with your unusual visualization. You want to travel and learn and will never know enough to suit you. Sexually, you're intense and can drown yourself in passion.

SEPTEMBER 14

You're a bit of a rebel, a colorful conversationalist, and always exactly who you are. Your mental skills find expression in projects others can't begin to think of. Love is a pivotal experience, for you are anything but casual.

SEPTEMBER 15

You're witty and quick on the mark, and you have a special skill for making others love you. Inwardly you worry about every imperfection, but people see someone irresistibly magnetic. In love, you have an aloof quality that hides a sensitive, easily affected heart.

SEPTEMBER 16

Though you're devoted to friendships and work commitments, you are an *explorer* who wants to keep moving to the next new adventure. You also enjoy solitude to do your own thing. Romantically, you are sensual and sentimental, and you need loyalty from a lover.

SEPTEMBER 17

You're a splendid communicator who can put across an idea. Others think of you as a people person and a mover and shaker, yet you see yourself as a lone artist. In love, you're passionate and enjoy intimacy, but lovers also call you crazy and hard to pin down.

SEPTEMBER 18

Ethical, responsible, and determined, you want to create something enduring (whether in work or family). Among the things most people don't see are your poetic imagination and ability to write, and the fact that you're easily hurt. You're also a secret romantic.

SEPTEMBER 19

You're fervent, restless, a visionary and humanitarian—and all this is contained within a charming persona. Still, you're stubborn about what you want, and your eclectic mind thinks out of the box. Emotionally, you can be a wanderer until you fall deeply in love.

SEPTEMBER 20

Courage runs through your veins, and you have faced challenges many have not. Your special destiny is to achieve unexpected fame. You have an independent spirit and a willingness to break out of boundaries. In love, you're highly intuitive and sexually expressive.

SEPTEMBER 21

Your personality has allure and magnetism, and your mind is quick and shrewd. More than this, you were born at a special time of inspiration and have unusual creative talent. In matters of the heart, you tend to sublimate your needs to those of your lover.

SEPTEMBER 22

Born on the last day of Virgo, you have unpredictable genius. You're a marvelous mix of sociability and charm, are an outspoken fast thinker, and have theatrical and literary ability. Deeply emotional but highly intellectual, you're also a dazzling flirt.

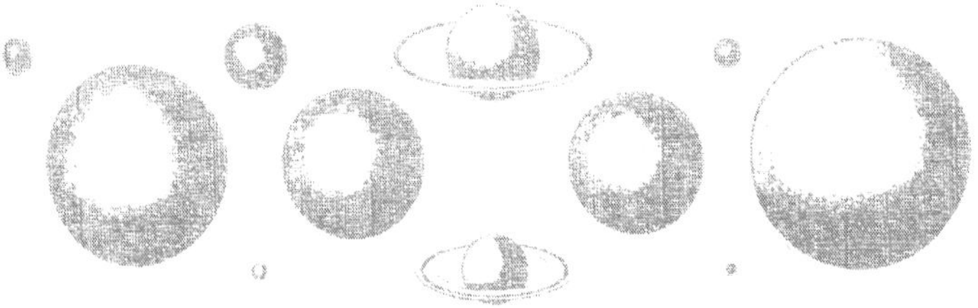

YOU AND CHINESE ASTROLOGY

With Marco Polo's adventurous travels in A.D. 1275, Europeans learned for the first time of the great beauty, wealth, history, and romance of China. Untouched as they were by outside influences, the Chinese developed their astrology along different lines from other ancient cultures, such as the Egyptians, Babylonians, and Greeks in whose traditions Western astrology has its roots. Therefore the Chinese zodiac differs from the zodiac of the West. To begin with, it's based on a lunar cycle rather than Western astrology's solar cycle. The Chinese zodiac is divided into twelve years, and each year is represented by a different animal—the rat, ox, tiger, rabbit, dragon, snake, horse, goat, monkey, rooster, dog, or pig. The legend of the twelve animals is that when Buddha lay on his deathbed, he asked the animals of the forest to come and bid him farewell. These twelve were the first to arrive. The cat, as the story goes, is not among the animals because it was napping and couldn't be bothered to make the journey. (In some Asian countries, however, such as Vietnam, the cat replaces the rabbit.)

Like Western astrology, in which the zodiac signs have different characteristics, each of the twelve Chinese animal years assigns character traits specific to a person born in that year. For example, the Year of the Rat confers honesty and an analytical mind, whereas the Year of the Monkey grants charm and a quick ability to spot opportunity.

Here are descriptions for Virgo for each Chinese animal year:

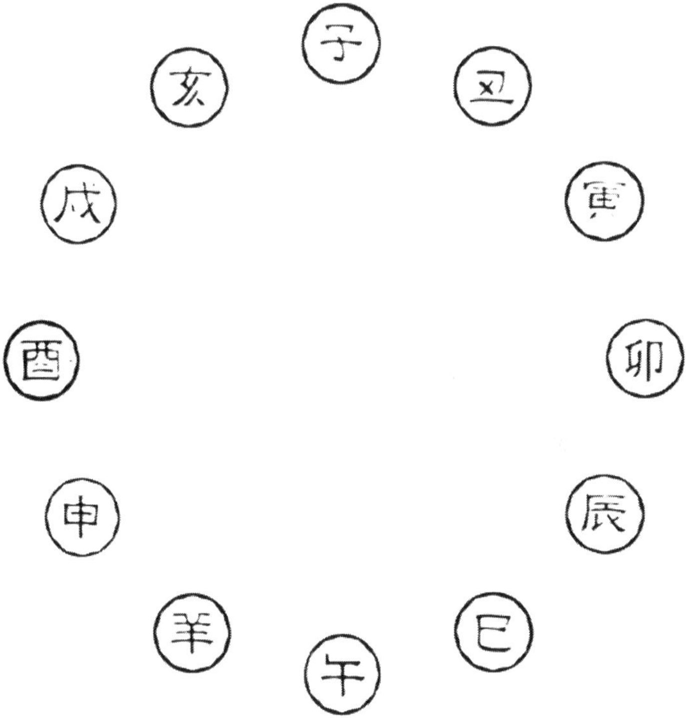

IF YOU ARE VIRGO BORN IN THE YEAR OF THE RAT

Years of the Rat

1900	1960	2020	2080
1912	1972	2032	2092
1924	1984	2044	
1936	1996	2056	
1948	2008	2068	

Unlike the lowly and repugnant Western rat, the Chinese Rat is said to be witty and resourceful and have sparkling charm. The Year of the Rat confers honest character and an analytic mind, qualities that magnify your Virgo refinement and conscientiousness. As a Virgo Rat you're blessed with great mental energy and creative talent. You're skilled at what you do and know how to communicate effectively. In particular, you're good at organizing a group and making wise executive decisions. However, you are a worrier who meddles too much in other people's affairs. You always know best—and it's true you really *do* know best, although this annoys others. In love, you're caring, sentimental, and sexually passionate. If you have a fault, it's that you're too forgiving. Lovers can take advantage of your loyal heart. Compatible partners are born in the Years of the Monkey, Pig, Rat, and Snake.

IF YOU ARE VIRGO BORN IN THE YEAR OF THE OX

Years of the Ox

1901	1961	2021	2081
1913	1973	2033	2093
1925	1985	2045	
1937	1997	2057	
1949	2009	2069	

The graceful, dignified Chinese Ox brings stability and equilibrium to whatever is disordered. Contrary to the image of a lumbering bovine creature, the Ox has polish, eloquence, and farsighted vision. Ox qualities of high intelligence and trustworthiness combine seamlessly with Virgo meticulousness and sense of responsibility. As a Virgo Ox, you're precise in your thinking and methodical in your habits. In addition, you are generous and giving emotionally. You reach out to others and can be quite self-sacrificing. In work, you're a good manager who inspires others and can handle money. In love, you're a romantic idealist—deeply passionate and utterly loyal. However, you do have to fight against stubbornness, rigidity, and becoming an autocrat. Don't let your Virgo tendency to carp get the upper hand. Compatible partners are born in the Years of the Rabbit, Rooster, Monkey, Pig, and Snake.

IF YOU ARE VIRGO BORN IN THE YEAR OF THE TIGER

Years of the Tiger

1902	1962	2022	2082
1914	1974	2034	2094
1926	1986	2046	
1938	1998	2058	
1950	2010	2070	

Symbolizing the power of faith, the Chinese Tiger is daring and magnetic, unafraid of any challenge. Asian teachings say the Tiger is a magnificent protector. Being born in the Year of the Tiger bestows dazzle—you have special radiance, irresistible attractiveness, and the ability to captivate an audience. Certainly, your creative talents are superior. You're also kindhearted and abundantly generous, and your Tiger magnanimity blends with your Virgo responsibility to others. Thus, as a Virgo Tiger, you're reliable and caring, filled with strong desire to fix the world. Indeed, the Year of the Tiger always ushers in "revolution," and at heart you're a rebel and instigator for positive change. True you can be short-tempered and have a way of not taking into account others' feelings. Still, in love, you're a firecracker—sexual and absurdly romantic. Compatible partners are born in the Years of the Rabbit, Dog, Dragon, Monkey, Pig, and Tiger.

IF YOU ARE VIRGO BORN IN THE YEAR OF THE RABBIT

Years of the Rabbit

1903	1963	2023	2083
1915	1975	2035	2095
1927	1987	2047	
1939	1999	2059	
1951	2011	2071	

The Chinese Rabbit is talented and communicative, endowed with people charisma and imagination. In parts of Asia (such as Vietnam), the Rabbit is known as the Cat, and you, born in this Year, have a talent for landing on your feet. Rabbit poise, style, and adaptability integrate beautifully with your Virgo brilliance, making you not only a scholar but also an adventurer, not just good at business but also a gifted artist. You are theatrical and ambitious, and you have an instinct for making money. You know how to get along with people, for you have a charming way with gossip and tidbits of information. You also can spot an advantage and are not above being devious. In love, you're flirtatious and playfully sexual, and you adore a romantic escapade. Because you don't trust easily, it may take a while to seriously give your heart away. Compatible partners are born in the Years of the Goat, Dog, Dragon, Snake, Horse, and Monkey.

IF YOU ARE VIRGO BORN IN THE YEAR OF THE DRAGON

Years of the Dragon

1904	1964	2024	2084
1916	1976	2036	2096
1928	1988	2048	
1940	2000	2060	
1952	2012	2072	

The Asian Dragon represents a magnificent life. The Dragon is dominant, forceful, and achieving. The Year of the Dragon always ushers in positive change and good fortune, and being born in a Dragon year promises that you will realize your ideals. Dragon strength and perseverance underline your Virgo willpower—you're able to see splendid possibilities to which others are blind. As a Virgo Dragon, you're gifted, intelligent, and tenacious, and you have irresistible magnetism. Yet sociable as you are, you do your most powerful original work when left alone to create. Some find you obstinate and somewhat of a braggadocio, but you're incapable of meanness. In love, you're sentimental and *seductive*—indeed, your sensuality can arouse jealousy. And your own high romantic expectations often lead to disillusionment with lovers who fail you. Compatible partners are born in the Years of the Rabbit, Goat, Monkey, Snake, and Tiger.

IF YOU ARE VIRGO BORN IN THE YEAR OF THE SNAKE

Years of the Snake

1905	1965	2025	2085
1917	1977	2037	2097
1929	1989	2049	
1941	2001	2061	
1953	2013	2073	

Unlike the Western snake who unpopularly connotes danger and deceit, the Asian Snake is aligned with the Goddess of Love and Beauty. The Year of the Snake confers elegance and brilliance, an imaginative aesthetic sense, and insight into the hearts of others. The Snake's refined perceptions only magnify your discriminating Virgo taste and spirit of service. As a Virgo Snake you're cerebral and give the impression of calm decisiveness. You're a psychologist, for you are understanding and compassionate while also making shrewd judgments about people. You're a good moneymaker, and can definitely be cunning and selfish. But you're so alluring that others are drawn to you, and you have powerful sexuality, especially in romantic affairs. In love, you tend to wander off the straight and narrow, though you yourself are quite possessive. Compatible partners are born in the Years of the Rabbit, Rooster, Dragon, Horse, Ox, and Rat.

IF YOU ARE VIRGO BORN IN THE YEAR OF THE HORSE

Years of the Horse

1906	1966	2026	2086
1918	1978	2038	2098
1930	1990	2050	
1942	2002	2062	
1954	2014	2074	

The Horse is among the most powerful Chinese astrological signs. It signifies the heroic and living an uncommon life, and it is so important that in Asia pregnancies are planned around the Year of the Horse. The Horse is magnetic and ambitious, a leader and rebel born to accomplish great deeds. Its driving force is to find freedom—of expression, career, and lifestyle, and also freedom geographically. You, born in the Year of the Horse, will always go your own way, and you thrive when you pursue your passion. This dedication to a goal enlarges your Virgo ability to see patterns, and, as a Virgo Horse, you have a genius for knowing how to run an enterprise. True, you can be hotheaded, impatient, and tactless, but you have honorable character. In love, you're a grand romantic who expects more of lovers than they can usually give. Ultimately, though, you're promised happiness. Compatible partners are born in the Years of the Rabbit, Rooster, Goat, Horse, and Snake.

IF YOU ARE VIRGO BORN IN THE YEAR OF THE GOAT

Years of the Goat

1907	1967	2027	2087
1919	1979	2039	2099
1931	1991	2051	
1943	2003	2063	
1955	2015	2075	

The Chinese Goat has charm and playfulness and an artistic turn of mind. In the midst of chaotic situations, the Goat can introduce inventive ideas about how to fix what's wrong. Basically, the Goat is a thinker and sage, and this added to your Virgo eye for detail and fertile imagination makes you a superb originator. You're always a fresh breeze of intelligence; the Chinese call you a "wayward artist." You also have a way of breezing onto a scene and then suddenly taking off (some would call you undisciplined). Actually, you suffer from lifelong dissatisfaction, and your wandering spirit tends to take you to unusual places and complicated emotional scenarios. In romance, you're sweetly sensitive and look for perfect love—yet your sexual seductiveness tangles up your affairs. You're a bit too trusting, as well, and may have your heart broken at least once. Compatible partners are born in the Years of the Rabbit, Dragon, Horse, Monkey, and Pig.

IF YOU ARE VIRGO BORN IN THE YEAR OF THE MONKEY

Years of the Monkey

1908	1968	2028	2088
1920	1980	2040	2100
1932	1992	2052	
1944	2004	2064	
1956	2016	2076	

The Asian Monkey is the merry companion of the God of Sailors, bringing cheer during long voyages. The Monkey is smart, quick, and adept at spotting opportunity, as well as very entertaining and charming, qualities that light up your Virgo brainpower. You can read people in an instant and dig out information almost psychically. You're also a wonderful "actor" who can adapt to any milieu in which you find yourself. You're the Virgo most skillful in public, a great advantage in career. Known for your style, wit, and taste, you're what others call an unforgettable character. You have superior intelligence and a bit of a wily streak. You can be devious, though Virgo ethics counterbalance this tendency. It's in the arena of love that your changeableness is most evident. You fall in love with total passion, but it takes an especially smart lover to keep you in thrall for the long haul. Compatible partners are born in the Years of the Rabbit, Dragon, Ox, Pig, Rat, and Tiger.

IF YOU ARE VIRGO BORN IN THE YEAR OF THE ROOSTER

Years of the Rooster

1909	1957	2005	2053
1921	1969	2017	2065
1933	1981	2029	2077
1945	1993	2041	2089

In Asian folklore the brave Rooster rescues the Goddess of the Sun, and thus is the symbol of courage. The Rooster is admired for its fortitude and pluck, and loved for its sincere heart. These sterling traits make your Virgo intelligence and capableness even more effective. People see you as a risk taker (perhaps it's your blind faith). Certainly, you have *bounce-back* ability, a priceless treasure you carry with you through an eventful life. Basically, you have enthusiasm for living and this, coupled with your kindness, makes you a joy to know. You're a style setter who is fond of novelty and new learning, and you have a multitude of talents. It's true you can be stubborn about doing things your way, especially in work, and you run the gamut between penny-pinching and extravagance. In love, you look for romance, passion, and sensuality, and often give up too much of yourself to keep the fantasy going. Compatible partners are born in the Years of the Horse, Ox, and Snake.

IF YOU ARE VIRGO BORN IN THE YEAR OF THE DOG

Years of the Dog

1910	1958	2006	2054
1922	1970	2018	2066
1934	1982	2030	2078
1946	1994	2042	2090

Dedicated and devoted, the Asian Dog (like its real life counterpart) symbolizes fidelity. The Year of the Dog always brings a cycle of reward for doing one's duty—and you born in this Year are destined to gain high prizes. The Dog is trustworthy in every sense of the word, which makes your Virgo sense of responsibility twice as achieving. You're the Virgo with shining ambitions, and you have a talent for taking on huge tasks and moving into positions of leadership. People rely on your integrity, and you inspire confidence. However, you are a worrier, and when stressed are sharp tongued and faultfinding. You can also turn cold and withdrawn. Mostly, though, you just want to be helpful, and you are tenderly caring, especially in love. When you're involved sexually, secret passions come to the fore and your jealousy is easily aroused. You need to learn how not to take things too much to heart. Compatible partners are born in the Years of the Rabbit, Dog, Pig, and Tiger.

IF YOU ARE VIRGO BORN IN THE YEAR OF THE PIG

Years of the Pig

1911	1959	2007	2055
1923	1971	2019	2067
1935	1983	2031	2079
1947	1995	2043	2091

In the West the pig ranks low on the Lovable Totem Pole, but the Asian Pig is held in high regard. The Pig is gallant, chivalrous, noble in spirit, and deeply loving. These elegant Pig qualities coupled with your superb Virgo taste and intelligence make you a person of refinement. You have discriminating judgment, are knowledgeable and creative, interested in the arts, and you support worthy causes. You have basic goodness of character, though oddly, for someone born with such a pure heart, you're destined to live an early life of vicissitudes. Still, you always arrive at the pot of gold, for you're hardworking and honest, brilliant in business, and clever with money. Love is where you really shine. In a much-too-casual world, you are the committed lover who gives of yourself emotionally and sexually. However, you must choose your partners carefully because others can easily take advantage of your trusting nature. Compatible partners are born in the Years of the Rabbit, Dog, Pig, and Tiger.

YOU AND NUMEROLOGY

Numerology is the language of numbers. It is the belief that there is a correlation between numbers and living things, ideas, and concepts. Certainly, numbers surround and infuse our lives (e.g., twenty-four hours in a day, twelve months of the year, etc.). And from ancient times mystics have taught that numbers carry a *vibration*, a deeper meaning that defines how each of us fits into the universe. According to numerology, you are born with a personal number that contains information about who you are and what you need to be happy. This number expresses what numerology calls your life path.

All numbers reduce to one of nine digits, numbers 1 through 9. Your personal number is based on your date of birth. To calculate your number, write your birth date in numerals. As an example, the birth date of August 26, 1984, is written 8-26-1984. Now begin the addition: 8 + 26 + 1 + 9 + 8 + 4 = 56; 56 reduces to 5 + 6 = 11; 11 reduces to 1 + 1 = 2. The personal number for someone born August 26, 1984, is *Two*.

IF YOU ARE A VIRGO ONE

Keywords: Confidence and Creativity

One is the number of leadership and new beginnings. You rush into whatever engages your heart, and tend to be more impulsive than many Virgos. You're courageous and inventive, and people respond to your decisiveness if not always to your impatience. You have a spirit of cooperation with people, but can't bear to be under anyone's whims and agendas. You want to keep learning, and to express who *you* are in work and relationships. Careers you do best in are those that allow you to work independently. In love, you want ecstasy and passion and, though you're loyal, the most exciting part of a flirtation is the beginning.

IF YOU ARE A VIRGO TWO

Keywords: Cooperation and Balance

Two is the number of cooperation and creating a secure entity. Being a Two gives you extra Virgo magnetism—you attract what you need. Your magic is your ability to breathe life into empty forms (e.g., a concept, an ambitious business idea, a new relationship) and produce something of worth. The work you do is always useful and you are a perfectionist. Because you have both a creative side *and* a practical side, you're drawn to careers that combine a business sense with an artistic challenge. In love, your deepest desire is for a loving partnership with someone you can trust and share confidences with.

IF YOU ARE A VIRGO THREE

Keywords: Expression and Sensitivity

Three symbolizes self-expression. You have a gift for words and a talent for visualization. You link people together so that they benefit from each other. You stimulate others to think. In career, you seek out ventures in which you use your mind fully and interact with those who match your intelligence. Because you're creative, you have a gift for bringing a touch of innovation to traditional ways of thinking. In love, you need someone who excites you intellectually and sensually, and who understand your complex personality. Casual acquaintances may not see your depth, but in love, you must have a soulmate who does.

IF YOU ARE A VIRGO FOUR

Keywords: Stability and Process

Four is the number of dedication and loyalty. It represents *foundation*, exactly as the four-sided square does that symbolizes Four. You are a builder, and the direction you go in is up. First you plan, then day-by-day you add the next step, the next layer, keeping on schedule. Your strength is that you're persistent and therefore you create worthy handiwork. Because you want to feel you can rely on yourself, you extend this to being responsible for others. In love, you look for a relationship with staying power. You need a faithful, giving and understanding lover with whom you can express your rich sensuality.

IF YOU ARE A VIRGO FIVE

Keywords: Freedom and Discipline

Five is the number of change and freedom. With your chameleon intellect (it can go in any direction) and ability to reach out to people, you're a marvelous *persuader*. More open-minded and independent than many Virgos, you want to learn all you can from a broad range of personalities and be free to pursue *your* choices. In relationships, you're a communicator who's quick to jump in to give advice (sometimes unasked for). In love, you need romantic fantasy but also want a partner who looks ahead to new goals. When you give your heart away it's to someone with whom you passionately mesh—body and mind.

IF YOU ARE A VIRGO SIX

Keywords: Vision and Acceptance

Six is the number of teaching, healing, and utilizing your talents. You're geared toward changing the world or at least fixing other people's lives. Being an advice-giver and even a therapist to your friends comes naturally. You're also competitive, exacting, and demanding—especially with yourself. You're your own harshest critic, for you hold yourself up to a standard of excellence. As a Virgo *perfector*, you'd like life to run like well-oiled machine. In love, you're fervent about being a helpmate and confidante, as well as a lover. You're also a secret sensualist who gives your all to someone you trust.

IF YOU ARE A VIRGO SEVEN

Keywords: Trust and Openness

Seven is the number of the mystic and the intensely focused specialist. You have an instinct for problem-solving, and in a flash understand how things work (in business, between people, etc.). You're an intellectual, a philosopher, and a connoisseur of everything creative. With your Virgo power of organization, you carve out your own territory. Your work, though, is only part of a deeper search for trust in yourself. At your core you're extremely loyal and intensely loving, though very selective about relationships. In love, your deepest need is for a partner who can help you in your journey to becoming the real you.

IF YOU ARE A VIRGO EIGHT

Keywords: Abundance and Power

Eight is the number of mastery and authority. You are intelligent, alert, quick in action, born to take power in your own hands and guide traffic into the direction you want. You work well in large groups because you see what's needed and can delegate (a major success tool). Others sense you're the one who knows best, and they're right. You tackle the hard stuff and never let anyone down. As a Virgo Eight, you're totally true to your word. Giving your promise in love is a very serious act. You are a protective and deeply caring lover, and in turn you need to know your lover is your unwavering ally.

IF YOU ARE A VIRGO NINE

Keywords: Integrity and Wisdom

Nine is the path of the "old soul," the number of completion and full bloom. Because it's the last number, it sums up the highs and lows of human experience, and you live a life of dramatic events. You're very intellectual, interested in exploring ideas, as well as deeply feeling and extremely protective. People see you as heroic because you have a forward-thinking outlook but are also spiritual and altruistic; at heart you're a humanitarian. In love, you're truthful and sincere—and also a romantic, highly sensual creature. As a Virgo Nine you generously give of yourself, often to the point of being sacrificing.

LAST WORD: YOUR VIRGO UNFINISHED BUSINESS

Psychologists often use the phrase *unfinished business* to describe unresolved issues—for example, patterns from childhood that cause unhappiness, anger that keeps one stuck, or scenarios of family dysfunction that repeat through second and third generations (such as alcoholism or abusive behavior).

Astrology teaches that the past is indeed very much with us in the present—and that using astrological insights can help us move out of emotional darkness into greater clarity. Even within this book (which is not a tome of hundreds of pages) you have read of many of the superlatives and challenges of being Virgo. You have breathtaking gifts, and at the same time certain tendencies that can undermine utilizing these abilities.

In nature, a fascinating fact is that in jungles and forests a poisonous plant will grow in a certain spot, and always just a few feet away is a plant that is the antidote to that specific poison. Likewise, in astrology, the antidote is right there, ready to be used when the negatives threaten to overwhelm your life.

Virgo's unfinished business has to do with feeling angry and powerless because the world does not recognize your worth. You are the one who does for others—you fulfill what they want of you. You expect appreciation; and when you keep trying harder to win approval and don't get it, you view the world as your enemy. You're the slave and "they" the master who makes drudgery and being overlooked your lot in life.

Like the other Earth signs (Taurus and Capricorn) you need structure and security, a sense of belonging. As a child, you probably sought approval by being the well-behaved one in the family, the studious student, and the cooperative friend. Yet from an early age Virgo tends to suffer from insecurity, a feeling of inferiority, and a fear of rejection. Other feelings pile on top of this: a sense of being excluded, being treated as a servant, being the loner. The mind spins into negativity, seeing others as stupid, rude, and ungrateful, seeing the world through a dark filter of resentment.

Both Virgo and Gemini are ruled by Mercury, planet of the mind and of ideas, and you both share the trait of identifying yourself with your ideas. Thus, if you believe others are callous and mean-spirited, you shut out other possibilities. Indeed, you have such a strong mind, you can actually bring about what you believe—your ideas become self-fulfilling. Your negativity breeds negativity around you. Being sour and turned-off result in others turning away from you.

It seems a cruel cosmic joke that you, who are so superior, should feel less-than, and that your Virgo skill for making sure things work correctly spills into worry that they won't. The more entrenched your pessimism becomes, the more overpowering your fear grows that something will go wrong or be taken away.

Yet the antidotes are there to be found in their entirety in being Virgo, for you are indeed superlative and far above the average—a person of *excellence* in every sense of the word. If anyone has the tools to live a fulfilling and impassioned life, it's you, Virgo. Your intellect is brilliant, and your heart is deeply caring. When you allow it to blossom, you also have a visionary sense twice as powerful as that of someone who isn't as grounded as you.

One reason you're such an exceptional manager (of concepts, people, systems) is you see from the outset how things can fit together to make flawless working order. You have a vision of possibility and, like a hero, you believe in the idea of perfection. You have kindness and commitment, and you *contribute*. You even have deep-down knowledge that you are gifted and superior—and somewhere, even in your darkest periods of insecurity, you can access this.

Another of your strengths is that you do keep on keeping on despite outside setbacks and inner angst. You're a good soldier who does your duty, but more than this you're a protector. A part of you really does care about others and care enough to make the world a better place—and the world truly needs you, Virgo.

Alongside your fussiness and insularity, your fear and resentment, exists a love for learning and a purity of motive. You're patient and enduring, and have the power to transform what you touch. On the highest level, your sign of Virgo represents healing and wholeness, and few are born with your great sense of purpose. Your unfinished business is to get past your Virgo anger and open your heart to love and work, to utilize your ability to put right the ills and malfunctions we human beings produce, to discover your Virgo incorruptibility.

FAMOUS PEOPLE WITH THE SUN IN VIRGO

Marc Antony
Yasir Arafat
Lance Armstrong
Lauren Bacall
Anne Bancroft
Ingrid Bergman
Leonard Bernstein
Jacqueline Bisset
Charles Boyer
Kobe Bryant
Sid Caesar
John Cage
Taylor Caldwell
Agatha Christie
Craig Claiborne
Patsy Cline
Confucius
Sean Connery
Harry Connick Jr.
Jimmy Connors
Jackie Cooper
Macaulay Culkin
Roald Dahl
Cameron Diaz
Theodore Dreiser
Queen Elizabeth I (the Virgin Queen)
Peter Falk
Greta Garbo
Richard Gere
Johann Wolfgang von Goethe
Hugh Grant
Buddy Hackett
O. Henry
Faith Hill
Jeremy Irons
Christopher Isherwood
Michael Jackson
Jesse James
Samuel Johnson
Tommy Lee Jones
Michael Keaton
Gene Kelly
Stephen King
Peter Lawford
D. H. Lawrence
Alan Jay Lerner
Rocky Marciano
Judith Martin (Miss Manners)
John McCain
Freddie Mercury
Grandma Moses
Paul Muni
Bob Newhart
Arnold Palmer
Itzhak Perlman
Regis Philbin
Ryan Phillippe
River Phoenix
Keanu Reeves
LeAnn Rimes
Cal Ripkin Jr.
Margaret Sanger
William Saroyan
Claudia Schiffer
Peter Sellers
Charlie Sheen
Upton Sinclair
Oliver Stone
Mother Teresa
Leo Tolstoy
Lily Tomlin
Shania Twain
George Wallace
H. G. Wells

VIRGO.
Pl. 21.
BOOTES
COMA BERENICES
MONS MÆNALUS
Denebola
Vindemiatrix
LEO
LIBRA
CRATER
CORVUS
Algorab
NOCTUA
HYDRA
E
W
S

PART TWO

ALL ABOUT YOUR SIGN OF VIRGO

VIRGO'S ASTROLOGICAL AFFINITIES, LINKS, AND LORE

SYMBOL: The Virgin (or Maiden)

Representing purity of motive, modesty, industriousness, and service of oneself and one's talents toward helping others. To the Romans she was Ceres, Goddess of the Harvest. The Egyptians linked her with Isis (Goddess of Motherhood and Fertility) and Maat (Goddess of Truth). The Virgin is usually pictured holding a sheaf of wheat that symbolizes the harvesting of ideas and skills and using these to benefit (nourish) the world. Wheat also represents the process of sifting out what is valuable and useful.

RULING PLANET: Mercury ☿

Ancient Roman god who was the messenger and go-between. The name Mercury comes from a Latin word meaning "commerce."

In Greek mythology, Mercury was known as Hermes, God of the "Persuasive Tongue." In astrology Mercury rules intelligence and reason, communication, speaking, writing, all forms of exchange of ideas and information, and travel. Its influence emphasizes quick cleverness and predisposes toward a high-strung temperament.

DOMINANT KEYWORD

I ANALYZE

GLYPH ♍

The symbol represents a Virgin, for it is a pictograph of the human reproductive organs closed and untouched. The glyph is a straight line connected to two curved lines, one of which is crossed. This represents wisdom tied to feeling and emotion, and crossed by practicality.

PART OF THE BODY RULED BY VIRGO: The Nervous System and the Intestines

Virgos are prone to illness caused by stress and nervous tension. They are particularly susceptible to ulcers and colitis.

LUCKY DAY: Wednesday

The day named for Mercury, ruler of Virgo. "Wednesday" comes from Old Norse words meaning "Woden's Day." (Woden was the god associated with Mercury.)

LUCKY NUMBERS: 5 and 3

Numerologically, 5 is the number of intelligence, curiosity, resourcefulness, and mental dexterity—and 3 is linked to communication, persuasiveness, generosity, and a commitment to making others happy. These qualities align with the nature of Virgo.

TAROT CARD: The Hermit

The card in the Tarot linked to Virgo is the Hermit. Ancient names for this card are Prophet of the Eternal and Magus of the Voice of Power. In the Tarot, this card signifies lighting the way through the darkness. It speaks of introspection, standing apart to make wise analysis of the situation, and being on the path of enlightenment. The Hermit points to attainment and harvesting the fruit of one's efforts. When this card turns up in a Tarot reading, it signifies the need to go within and discover what it is you truly want; its deeper message is you need to know yourself well. Often it points to meeting someone who will guide you.

The card itself pictures a robed figure of an elderly man standing on a snowy mountaintop and holding a lantern that contains a radiant six-sided star. The figure of the Hermit represents absolute wisdom, and his lantern is the lamp of truth.

For Virgo, the Hermit tells you that you hold within yourself deep understanding. When you live from your values, you know the secrets of the universe—and your life's purpose is to bring this wisdom to others.

MAGICAL BIRTHSTONE: Sapphire

The gemstone that symbolizes purity, faith, and hope. Sapphires come in many colors but the most valuable are blue. From ancient times, the sapphire was linked to the blue of heaven and prized as an ecclesiastical ornament because it promotes a state of meditative contemplation. In many cultures it has been used as an amulet and thought to clarify the mind, aid in sleep, and cure eye problems. The star sapphire (a special sapphire in which a star is visible) carries the three qualities of faith, hope, and destiny. For Virgos, the sapphire is said to dispel melancholy, cheer the soul, bring tranquility of mind, and protect against illness and injury while traveling.

SPECIAL COLORS: Navy Blue, Gray, and Dark Brown

Classic colors of refinement, taste, and stability.

CONSTELLATION OF VIRGO

The star grouping of Virgo is the second largest in the heavens. In Babylonian times it was called the Furrow because it represented the harvest, specifically the trench made by a plow in which corn and grain grow. The brightest star in Virgo is called Spica, which is the Latin word for "ear of grain." Schoolchildren learn to identify Virgo by finding Spica ("follow the arc to Arcturus and speed on to Spica"). Virgo is linked to Isis and Maat (Egyptian goddesses of protection and of truth), to Demeter (Greek goddess of agriculture), and to Ceres (Roman goddess of fertility and the harvest). The Sun journeys through the constellation of Virgo at harvest time, before the arrival of autumn, and from antiquity has been associated with fertility, growth, and abundance.

CITIES

Paris, Boston, Athens, Heidelberg, Strasbourg

COUNTRIES

New Zealand, Turkey, Greece, Brazil, West Indies

FLOWERS

Morning Glory and Pansy

TREES

Nut-bearing trees

HERBS AND SPICES

Tumeric and Saffron

METAL: Mercury

Named for the god Mercury who governed mobility, speed, and communication. The written symbols for the planet Mercury (ruler of Virgo) and the metal mercury are the same. Mercury is one of only four metals that are liquid at room temperature. In this state mercury is known as "quicksilver," which suggests the quick-moving quality of thoughts and ideas. In ancient times, alchemists believed mercury was capable of changing into other metals, such as gold. The resulting symbolism is that mercury, representing knowledge of the mind, can be transformed into understanding of the heart.

ANIMALS RULED BY VIRGO

Small domestic pets

DANGER

Virgo people sometimes arouse anger and violence in others because of their tendency to interfere, their critical tongues, and their unemotional attitudes.

PERSONAL PROVERB

There is no such thing in your life as an unimportant day.

KEYWORDS FOR VIRGO

Intelligent
Altruistic
Hard worker
Honest
Practical
Curious
Efficient
Organized
Responsible
Devotion to duty
Taking pains to be accurate
Perfectionist
Tidy
Good teacher
Healer
Humane
Exacting
Critical
Nitpicking
Demanding
Detail-obsessed
Precise

Worrier
Nervous
Hyperenergetic
Health-conscious

HOW ASTROLOGY SLICES AND DICES YOUR SIGN OF VIRGO

DUALITY: Feminine

The twelve astrological signs are divided into two groups, *masculine* and *feminine*. Six are masculine and six are feminine; this is known as the sign's *duality*. A masculine sign is direct and energetic. A feminine sign is receptive and magnetic. These attributes were given to the signs about 2,500 years ago. Today modern astrologers avoid the sexism implicit in these distinctions. A masculine sign does not mean "positive and forceful" any more than a feminine sign means "negative and weak." In modern terminology, the masculine signs are defined as outer-directed and strong through action. The feminine signs, such as your sign of Virgo, are self-contained and strong through inner reserves.

TRIPLICITY (ELEMENT): Earth

The twelve signs are also divided into groups of three signs. Each of these three-sign groups is called a *triplicity*, and each of these denotes an *element*. The elements are *Fire*, *Earth*, *Air*, and *Water*. In astrology, an element symbolizes a fundamental characterization of the sign.

The three *Fire* signs are Aries, Leo, and Sagittarius. Fire signs are active and enthusiastic.

The three *Earth* signs are Taurus, Virgo, and Capricorn. Earth signs are practical and stable.

The three *Air* signs are Gemini, Libra, and Aquarius. Air signs are intellectual and communicative.

The three *Water* signs are Cancer, Scorpio, and Pisces. Water signs are emotional and intuitive.

QUADRUPLICITY (QUALITY): Mutable

The twelve signs are also divided into groups of four signs. Each of these four-sign groups is called a *quadruplicity*, and each of these denotes a *quality*. The qualities are *Cardinal*, *Fixed*, and *Mutable*. In astrology, the quality signifies the sign's interaction with the outside world.

Four signs are *Cardinal** signs. These are Aries, Cancer, Libra, and Capricorn. Cardinal signs are enterprising and outgoing. They are the initiators and leaders.

Four signs are *Fixed*. These are Taurus, Leo, Scorpio, and Aquarius. Fixed signs are resistant to change. They hold on; they are perfectors and finishers, rather than originators.

*When the Sun crosses the four cardinal points in the zodiac, we mark the beginning of each of our four seasons. Aries begins spring; Cancer begins summer; Libra begins fall; Capricorn begins winter.

Four signs are *Mutable*. These are Gemini, Virgo, Sagittarius, and Pisces. Mutable signs are flexible, versatile, and adaptable. They are able to adjust to differing circumstances.

Your sign of Virgo is a Feminine, Earth, Mutable sign—and no other sign in the zodiac is this exact combination. Your sign is a one-of-a-kind combination, and therefore you express the characteristics of your duality, element, and quality differently from any other sign.

For example, your sign is a *Feminine* sign, meaning you are receptive, caring, and resourceful. You're an *Earth* sign, meaning you're enduring, practical, and stable. And you're a *Mutable* sign, meaning you're able to go with the flow, adjust to changing circumstances, and take advantage of new situations.

Now, the sign of Taurus is also Feminine and Earth; but unlike Virgo (which is Mutable), Taurus is Fixed. Like you, Taurus is caring, nurturing, and practical—but Taurus is focused on keeping the status quo and resistant to change. Taurus can get very stuck; it doesn't have your openness to new ways of thinking. Taurus's motivation is to avoid risk and preserve what has been tested by time. It easily becomes opinionated, inflexible, and habit-bound. You, being Mutable, have a questioning mind that likes new learning, will experiment with ideas, and will adopt methods that produce results. Being such a mental person you enjoy testing various ways and means to find out what works. Your mutability gives you broader vision than a Taurus, and you enjoy exploring some side-paths to see what suits your purposes.

Capricorn, too, is Feminine and Earth, but unlike Virgo (which is Mutable), Capricorn is Cardinal. Like you, Capricorn is a dedicated doer who wants to make use of its talents and create sturdy structures. However, being Cardinal, Capricorn is drawn to the limelight, is more headstrong and ambitious, and seeks to break new ground. Its motivation is to take on power and be looked up to. You, being Mutable, are more able to flow into others' needs rather than use people as an audience. You have Mutable flexibility—a clever, fast-thinking approach that looks to the future and is oriented toward a result. In a project, for example, your interest is in making sure all the parts (and ideas) work together.

POLARITY: Pisces

The twelve signs are also divided into groups of two signs. Each of these two-sign groups is called a *polarity* (meaning "opposite"). Each sign in the zodiac has a polarity, which is its opposite sign in the other half of the zodiac. The two signs express opposite characteristics.

Virgo and Pisces are a polarity. Virgo is the sign of usefulness and industriousness. It governs the concept of *service*—serving your talents to their full potential, and serving the world to make it a better place. You are happiest when in the flow of making things work. You dissect facts to discover the truth. You find joy in the detail, and especially are most fulfilled when your efforts improve others' lives.

As a fixer, however, your focus can narrow down to improving the little thing and lose sight of the big picture. Virgo finds it easy to mend the patches and not get around to putting them back together into a quilt. Also, you're geared to how something can be of actual *use*, and will dismiss what you call far-out suggestions because they "just don't apply."

Pisces, your opposite sign, is the sign of dreams and imagination, intuition, and mysticism. Pisceans are supremely creative (although it's true they don't have your practicality). Inspiration and subjectivity are apt descriptions of the Piscean experience, for Pisces receives intuitive flashes of knowledge (seemingly from the universe) and also knows things intuitively from the heart. Experiences are all filtered through the emotions, and Pisces will look for the deeper meaning. With people, Pisces can be almost telepathic, seeing beneath the surface to what another is thinking. This is the sign of merging—emotionally and spiritually—and one of Pisces's strongest motivations is to be in close bonds.

Astrologically, you as a Virgo can benefit from adopting some of Pisces's emotionalism, empathy, and intuitive sense. You are a rationalist—you analyze, dissect, pick apart. You trust your head more than your heart. You're sensitive and loving, but uncomfortable with too much emotion and certainly with ambiguity. You're a perfectionist and a critical taskmaster. When people turn away from your disapproval, you feel unappreciated for your faithful service.

By tapping into Pisces's ability to blend with others on a heart level, you will be more valued and cared for, more involved. You are a caregiver, but you, too, need nurturing. By connecting more deeply, you'll receive the emotional support you need. Instead of feeling oppressed by duties, you can spend time enjoying, inventing, having fun (which Pisces does so well). By letting your imagination loose and listening to your feelings (not just what you're thinking or analyzing), you have the capacity to be a great visionary.

In turn, Pisces has much to learn from you, and at the top of this list is not wasting oneself. Pisces can easily lose its way in unrealistic dreams and fritter away its talents. Pisces is prone to self-delusion and escapism and wastes itself taking the easy way out. Like you, Pisces has a sensitive heart and is a giver, but squanders its emotional gifts because it can't set boundaries. By looking to you, Virgo, Pisces can learn that accomplishment means doing the work. That well-being of the mind, body, and spirit takes discipline and valuing oneself. That being neurotically self-sacrificing is self-destructive. And, especially, that one's values are shown in positive deeds, not vague fantasies and codependency.